A Prayer for You, Dear Reader

Before you begin this journey…

Father God,

I lift up the heart of the one holding this workbook right now. You see every wound, every question, every tear that may not have been seen or understood by others. But You know. And You care.

I ask that as they walk through these pages, You would walk beside them — comforting, guiding, and restoring. Let this journey be a sacred space where shame is silenced, truth is revealed, and Your love is made undeniably real.

Where there is confusion, bring clarity.
Where there is fear, bring peace.
Where there is pain, bring healing.
Where there is loss, bring new life.

May every word in this workbook lead them closer to You — not just to answers, but to Your presence.
Help them leave well — not with bitterness, but with peace.
Help them heal deeply — not just on the surface, but in the soul.

And when they are ready, Father, lead them to a Christ-centered community that reflects Your heart — full of grace, truth, and love.

In Jesus' name,

Amen.

"But blessed is the one who trusts in the Lord, whose confidence is in Him. They will be like a tree planted by the water that sends out its roots by the stream. It does not fear when heat comes; its leaves are always green. It has no worries in a year of drought and never fails to bear fruit." **Jeremiah 17:7–8**

Published by Victoria Russo
First Edition: 2025

Disclaimer

This book is for informational and inspirational purposes only. It is not intended as a substitute for professional counseling, therapy, or pastoral guidance. The experiences and insights shared in this book are based on the author's personal journey and research.

For permissions, inquiries, or speaking engagements, contact: info@truthwoven.com

Printed in the United States of America

ISBN: ISBN: 979-8998598906
Truthwoven Ministries

Scripture Acknowledgment

Unless otherwise noted, all Scripture quotations are taken from:

New International Version (NIV), © 1973, 1978, 1984, 2011 by Biblica, Inc. Used by permission. All rights reserved worldwide.

English Standard Version (ESV), © 2001, 2006, 2011, 2016 by Crossway Bibles, a publishing ministry of Good News Publishers. Used by permission. All rights reserved.

New Living Translation (NLT), © 1996, 2004, 2015 by Tyndale House Foundation. Used by permission. All rights reserved.

King James Version (KJV) – Public Domain.

Table of Contents

Leaving Well, *Healing* Deep
When Church Culture Hurts

———————— ✦ ————————

Healing Workbook to Recognize Church Hurt, Uncover Toxic Culture, and Rebuild Trust in Christ and Community

PART OF THE FAITH AFTER CHURCH HURT SERIES

A Word of Thanks

To the church that first showed me what healthy, Spirit-led leadership looks like—thank you.

Your example taught me how to recognize truth, grace, and integrity within the body of Christ. Not long ago, I walked through a season that revealed what the church was never meant to be. But it was your foundation of love, wisdom, and biblical truth that helped me discern the difference.

Today, I'm honored to be back—serving, growing, and helping others heal in the very place that once helped shape my own faith.

You didn't just welcome me once. You welcomed me again—with open arms and unwavering grace.

I'm grateful for the way you continue to reflect the heart of Jesus—and for the opportunity to walk alongside others as they find their way back to Him.

"Now may the God of peace Himself sanctify you completely."

1 Thessalonians 5:23

How to Use This Workbook

This book is more than just words on a page—it is a journey of healing, a space for reflection, and an invitation to walk closely with God as He leads you toward freedom. As you read, I encourage you to pause, pray, and invite the Holy Spirit to guide you through each step.

This workbook is designed to help you process your experiences, reflect deeply, and seek God's direction. Healing is not a one-size-fits-all journey, but God is faithful to meet you where you are. Each chapter contains reflection questions, journaling prompts, and prayers intended to help you process your emotions and lean into God's love.

How to Engage with This Workbook:

1. **Pray Before You Begin** – Ask the Holy Spirit to speak to you as you go through this journey. Lean into His wisdom and let Him reveal the truth to you.

(**John 16:13** *"But when He, the Spirit of truth, comes, He will guide you into all the truth."*)

2. **Write From the Heart**– Be honest with yourself. Healing begins with acknowledging your emotions. You don't have to have all the answers—this is a space for grace.

3. **Take Your Time** – There is no rush. Healing is a process, and it unfolds in God's perfect timing. Allow yourself to sit with each section, process it fully, and return when needed.

4. **Use a Separate Journal** (Optional) – If you're reading the digital version of this book, Consider using a notebook or journal to write out your reflections and prayers.

5. **Invite God into Every Step** – You are not alone. Let God Walk with you through this process. His love, grace, and healing are available to you. (**Psalm 34:18** *"The Lord is close to the brokenhearted and saves those who are crushed in spirit."*)

No matter where you are on this journey, know that God sees you, He loves you, and He is guiding you. You are not alone, and your healing matters. My prayer is that this book will be a safe space for you to process, heal, and step into the freedom God has for you.

Dear Reader,

If you're holding this book, you may be carrying a weight that words can hardly describe. Maybe you've felt unseen, unheard, or even betrayed by a place that was meant to bring healing. Maybe you've wrestled with doubts—about your faith, your worth, or the path forward.

I know what that feels like. For a long time, I stayed in an environment that didn't feel like home. I was loyal—not to a church family, but to an organization. I convinced myself that my role and responsibilities mattered more than my discomfort. I kept showing up. But deep down, something didn't feel right.

Over time, the red flags became impossible to ignore. Leadership dismissed concerns, and I started doubting myself—*Was I being too critical? Was I expecting too much?* Yet the more I prayed, the clearer it became: I had to leave.

Walking away wasn't easy. It meant uncertainty and fear. But as I clung to God, He reminded me that my faith was never meant to be built on a church, a leader, or an organization. It belongs to Jesus alone.

The good news is, healthy churches do exist—communities that reflect Christ's love, grace, and truth. I know this firsthand.

I left my healthy home church after receiving what I believed was a great opportunity. But what seemed like an open door led me into a toxic environment. The red flags were clear—lack of accountability, lack of transparency, unresolved conflict, controlling leadership, manipulation, and a culture that prioritized loyalty over biblical truth.

Thankfully, because of the strong biblical foundation I had received in my home church, I was able to recognize the warning signs much sooner. Even though the experience was painful, it reassured me that not all churches are unhealthy. There are still Christ-centered, life-giving communities where people genuinely seek God.

I wrote this book for you—the one struggling to leave, to heal, to believe there is hope on the other side of faith-related pain. I want you to know that you are not alone. God has not abandoned you, and healing is possible.

This book is your invitation to healing—a guide to recognizing unhealthy church environments, walking away with courage, and rebuilding your faith on the unshakable foundation of Christ.

Wherever you are in your journey, I pray that these pages bring you clarity, peace, and the courage to embrace the freedom God has for you.

You are deeply loved, and your faith is worth fighting for.

Blessings,

Victoria Russo

Acknowledgments

First and foremost, I give all thanks and glory to God. Through this season, I have come out stronger—not because of my own strength, but because of His unwavering faithfulness.
In the moments when I felt lost, uncertain, or broken, He never left me. I now understand that sometimes we must walk through the fire to experience true healing and transformation. Even in the midst of pain, God's grace was there—leading me forward, restoring my faith, and reminding me that I was never alone.

To my husband and children—you are my greatest blessing. Your love, support, and sacrifice mean more to me than words can express. You believed in me, stood by me, and walked this journey with me, even when it meant making difficult choices. Your strength, patience, and encouragement gave me the courage to keep moving—especially when it felt impossible.

To my two dearest friends, my sisters in Christ—you know who you are. Your presence in my life has been a gift beyond measure. Thank you for your wise counsel, for walking alongside me through life's ups and downs, and for being a source of encouragement, truth, and steadfast support. Your prayers, wisdom, and love have carried me through some of my hardest moments. Your guidance during the writing of this book was invaluable. I am forever grateful for our friendship, our sisterhood, and the way you reflect Christ's love in all that you do.

To a wise and gracious mentor who came alongside me during this season—thank you for your insight, encouragement, and faithful support. Your wisdom, discernment, and willingness to speak truth in love gave me the courage to press forward in writing this book. I am deeply grateful for the time you invested in reading, editing, and offering thoughtful input. Your presence was a God-send in this process, and your guidance helped shape these pages into something I pray will bring healing to many.

God, my family, and the community He has placed around me mean everything to me. This book would not exist without the love, wisdom, and support that surrounded me in this season—from my loved ones, my dear friends, and those who have walked alongside me in faith. Your encouragement and prayers have been a source of strength, and I am forever grateful.

To every reader who picks up this book—you are seen, you are valued, and you are deeply loved. Your story matters. Your healing matters. May these pages bring you hope, clarity, and the courage to step into the freedom and faith that God has for you.

With love and gratitude,

V. Russo

Dedication

This book is dedicated to you—if you've ever felt unseen, misunderstood, or alone in your journey through faith-related pain. Your pain is valid, your experiences matter, and your voice deserves to be heard. May you find comfort, healing, and courage in these pages, knowing that you're not alone and your story holds incredible value.

Preface

This book was written for those who have experienced the pain of unhealthy church leadership and culture. Many struggle silently, burdened by fear, guilt, or the potential loss of community. My hope is that these pages will provide clarity, healing, and encouragement for those who feel trapped in toxic religious environments.

You deserve a faith built on the truth, grace, and love of Christ—not fear, control, or manipulation. Whether you are questioning, leaving, or healing, know this: God sees you, He has not abandoned you, and healing is possible.

Introduction: When Church Hurts More Than It Heals

Leaving a church is one of the most difficult spiritual decisions a person can make—especially when that church has been a significant part of their life. It is important to be able to recognize if your church is causing you more harm than good so you know when it is time to leave.

Have you ever asked yourself any of these questions?

Is your church causing more harm than good?
Do you feel like your faith is a burden?
Does leadership foster control rather than care?
Is your church pain drowning out your relationship with Christ?
Do you long for a Christian community but feel overwhelmed by fear?
Are you ready to begin the healing process and reclaim your peace?

If you answered *yes* to any of these questions, you are not alone. Many wrestle with guilt and uncertainty, asking: *Am I being disloyal to God? What will happen to my faith?* These are valid concerns, and this book will walk with you through them.

For many, church hurt happens because their faith was placed in a pastor, a community, or the church itself rather than in Christ. When we build our foundation on people, disappointment is inevitable—because people are imperfect. Leaders fail, churches make mistakes, and people can wound others, even in the name of God. But when our foundation is in Christ alone, we remain unshaken, no matter what happens around us.

However, a toxic church environment is different—it is a form of spiritual abuse that creates an unhealthy church experience. Unlike ordinary church conflicts, toxic churches often manipulate, control, and foster fear instead of faith. They prioritize power over people, distort Scripture for their own gain, and leave many questioning their worth, their faith, and even God Himself.

"By the grace God has given me, I laid a foundation as a wise builder, and someone else is building on it. But each one should build with care. For no one can lay any foundation other than the one already laid, which is Jesus Christ." **1 Corinthians 3:10-11**

Your faith is not dependent on a single church—it belongs to Christ alone. The journey ahead is one of healing, restoration, and rediscovering faith beyond toxicity. Together, we will explore how to:

- **Recognize unhealthy church environments**
- **Take steps toward leaving with wisdom**
- **Heal from spiritual wounds**
- **Rebuild trust and find a healthy, Christ-centered community**

If you feel stuck in a harmful church situation, know this: God sees you. He has not abandoned you. Healing is possible.

CHAPTER ONE

———— ◆ ————

WHEN CHURCH CULTURE BECOMES HARMFUL

"THEN YOU WILL KNOW THE TRUTH,
AND THE TRUTH WILL SET YOU FREE."

JOHN 8:32

When Church Culture Becomes Harmful

You may have sat in church, feeling uneasy, yet convinced yourself you were overthinking it. Maybe leadership dismissed concerns, or you feared speaking up. **You are not alone.** Many have walked this road, struggling to reconcile their faith with an unhealthy church culture.

Not All Church Hurt Is the Same

Churches, like any community, will have disagreements. A difficult season, a misunderstanding, or a leadership decision you don't agree with doesn't automatically mean a church is unhealthy. But when questioning is discouraged, control is disguised as 'spiritual authority,' and fear replaces grace, the environment has become toxic.

Church Hurt vs. Church Toxicity

There's a difference between **Church Hurt** and **a Toxic Church Culture**.

- **Church hurt** can result from human imperfections—misunderstandings, disappointments, or conflicts that can be resolved through healthy conversations and biblical reconciliation.
- **A toxic church culture** is different. It prioritizes power over people, silences concerns, distorts Scripture to maintain control, and fosters fear instead of faith.

So how do you know if your experience is just **church hurt** or something more serious? One key indicator is **spiritual abuse**.

What Is Spiritual Abuse?

Spiritual abuse is one of the most overlooked yet deeply painful forms of harm within the church. It doesn't always begin with obvious red flags—it often starts subtly, with a shift in focus away from Christ and toward control, performance, or unquestioned loyalty to leadership. Over time, this type of culture distorts truth, diminishes grace, and leads people to question their worth, their calling, and sometimes even their faith.

If you've ever felt confused, silenced, or ashamed in a church setting for simply asking questions, using your voice, or seeking accountability, you may have encountered spiritual abuse.

This section isn't about blame, it's about clarity. It's about helping you put words to what you may have experienced, and giving you the courage to identify patterns that don't reflect the heart of Christ.

Jesus came to set the captives free, not to place more burdens on their backs. He leads with humility, truth, and compassion. Spiritual abuse, on the other hand, often hides behind religious language but bears no resemblance to the character of Jesus. Let's break it down clearly so you can begin to recognize what's healthy and what's not because your healing starts with truth.

Signs of Spiritual Abuse:

1. **Controlling Leadership** – Leaders demand absolute loyalty and discourage questioning.

"Jesus led with humility, not control." **(Mark 10:42-45)**

2. **Legalism & Rule-Based Faith** –Emphasis on man-made rules over God's grace, leading to judgment and shame.

"We are saved by grace, not legalism." **(Ephesians 2:8-9)**

3. **Silencing Concerns**– Those who question or report issues are shamed, dismissed, or punished.

"Jesus defended and uplifted the hurting." **(Luke 4:18)**

4. **Twisting Scripture** – Bible verses are misused to control, manipulate, or justify mistreatment

"God's Word should bring truth and freedom." **(Matthew 4:1-11)**

5. **Poor Financial Stewardship**- Church funds are mismanaged, misused, or lack accountability.

"Resources should be handled with integrity." **(2 Corinthians 8:20-21)**

6. **Secrecy & Lack of Transparency**- Leadership hides financial records or major decisions from members.

"Jesus valued truth and openness." **(Proverbs 31:8-9)**

Why This Matters

These signs may not always appear all at once, but even one or two can create an unhealthy spiritual environment. The danger lies in how easily these patterns can be dismissed as "normal," especially when wrapped in spiritual language. But Jesus never manipulated, shamed, or hid behind authority—He served in love, led with integrity, and spoke truth even when it was uncomfortable.

If any of these patterns feel familiar to you, it doesn't mean you're weak in faith—it means you're discerning. Naming these behaviors is not dishonoring to the church; it's honoring the truth. And truth is where healing begins.

The Emotional Impact of Recognizing Spiritual Abuse

Realizing that you are in a toxic church environment can feel like the ground beneath you is crumbling. If you have experienced a healthy, Christ-centered church before, the red flags may be easier to recognize. But if a toxic church is all you've ever known, this realization can feel deeply unsettling—almost like waking up to a truth you were never allowed to question.

You may experience a whirlwind of emotions:

- **Denial:** *"Maybe I'm just overthinking things. No church is perfect."*
- **Guilt & Shame:** *"I should have known better. Maybe this is my fault."*
- **Fear:** *"If I leave, will I be abandoning God? What if they were right about me?"*
- **Confusion:** *"I don't even know what's true anymore. Who can I trust?"*
- **Anger & Betrayal:** *"How could people who claim to follow Christ act this way?"*
- **Grief & Loss:** *"I'm losing my community, my friends, my church family."*
- **Hope & Relief:** *"Maybe this is the first step toward real freedom in Christ."*

All of these emotions are completely normal. Healing begins when you acknowledge them, rather than suppress them. But no matter how painful this process feels—God is still present.

God Never Wastes Anything

Even in the midst of confusion, God is working. Even when you feel alone, Jesus is walking beside you **(Deuteronomy 31:8)**. What the enemy meant for harm, God can use for good if we give him the broken pieces of our faith. **(Genesis 50:20).**

- If you've been hurt in the church, ***God can bring healing***.
- If you've been deceived, ***God can restore the truth***.
- If you've been spiritually wounded, ***God can restore your soul***.

    "Jesus Himself will bind up those wounds." **Psalm 147:3.**

God never wastes anything—not even our pain. Even if you've only ever known a toxic church culture, He can redeem your story, restore your faith, and lead you into a healthy, Christ-centered community where you can thrive.

You are not alone in this journey. Jesus is your guide, your protector, and your firm foundation.

Isaiah 41:10 *"So do not fear, for I am with you; do not be dismayed, for I am your God. I will strengthen you and help you; I will uphold you with my righteous right hand."*

As we move forward in this journey, we'll discuss how to leave well, how to heal, and how to rebuild your faith stronger than before, anchored in Christ alone.

But before we can move forward, it's important to pause and honestly acknowledge what may have caused harm.On the next page, you'll find a list of common warning signs that may indicate toxic church culture or spiritual manipulation. Recognizing what was not of God is a powerful step toward healing in Him.

Warning Signs of an unhealthy Church

You may not be sure if what you are experiencing is unhealthy, take a moment and review some of the examples provided. If you have ever experienced any of these warning signs, it is possible you might be in an unhealthy church environment.

Examples of possible warning signs

Authoritarian Leadership	Guilt & shame for questioning anything
Lack of Transparency	Conditional love and acceptance
Prioritizes growth/finances over spiritual well-being	Excessive control of doctrine
Us vs Them Mentality	Shunning and ostracism
Emotional or spiritual manipulation	Financial Exploitation
Legalistic teachings	Control over personal life
Lack of accountability in leadership	Isolation from outside opinion
Suppression of concerns	Spiritual intimidation
Values do not match actions	Punishing dissent
Prioritizes rules over people	Spiritual gaslighting

Processing:

If you found yourself identifying with any of the warning signs listed above, take a moment and breathe. Sometimes, simply naming what you've experienced is the first act of healing. It's not always easy to admit that a place we trusted may not have been spiritually healthy. But acknowledging truth is not a sign of rebellion—it's a step toward restoration.

You may feel confused, relieved, overwhelmed, or unsure. That's okay.

This is not about blaming or pointing fingers—it's about recognizing what's not aligned with God's heart, so you can step into freedom, clarity, and healing. The Holy Spirit brings conviction, not confusion. He leads with peace, not pressure.

Free Journal Page:

(Use this space to write freely. There's no right or wrong way to process your story. Just be honest. God meets you in the details.)

_____

_____

_____

_____

_____

_____

_____

_____

_____

_____

_____

_____

_____

_____

_____

_____

_____

_____

What's Next?

Recognizing that you are in a toxic church is the first step toward freedom, but it's not the end of the journey. Now what?

Once you realize that something is deeply wrong, emotions may begin to surface—grief, anger, fear, confusion, even relief. It can feel like everything you believed is unraveling.

But remember this: **God is still with you.** He is not afraid of your questions, your emotions, or your struggles. The process of leaving a toxic church is not just about walking away from something unhealthy—it's about walking toward healing in Christ.

Before we move into the next chapter, you'll find a set of guided reflection questions designed to help you process your experience and gently invite God into the places that still hurt. These prompts aren't meant to judge or diagnose—but to help you untangle your story with honesty, grace, and clarity. Go slow. Pray as you go. God is near—and He is faithful.

As you finish these reflections, take a deep breath. When you're ready, we'll keep moving—together.

In the next chapter, we'll explore the emotional and spiritual impact of leaving—why it feels so heavy, how to process your emotions in a healthy way, and how to hold onto God's truth through it all.

Reflection Questions:

1. Have you ever noticed warning signs in a church that made you feel uneasy?

Answer: _____

_____

_____

_____

2. What emotions arise when you think about your past church experiences?

Answer: _____

_____

_____

_____

3. Have you ever been made to feel guilty for asking questions about church practices?

Answer: _____

_____

_____

_____

4. In what ways have you witnessed or experienced any of the examples provided?

Answer: _____

_____

_____

_____

Journaling Exercise: Identifying Toxicity in Your Church

1. Have you ever been discouraged from asking questions or expressing doubts? What happened?

Answer: _____

_____

_____

_____

2. Have you ever felt pressured to stay silent about something that felt wrong?

Answer: _____

_____

_____

_____

3. How did your church leaders respond when people disagreed with them?

Answer: _____

_____

_____

_____

4. One of the biggest lessons I've learned about my church culture is:

Answer: _____

_____

_____

_____

Prayer for Clarity & Discernment

Lord, open my eyes to see the truth. Give me discernment to recognize what is from You and what is not. Protect my heart from manipulation and lead me into Your freedom. Amen.

Journaling & Prayer Reflection

At the end of each chapter, take a moment to pause and reflect. Use this space to write down what stood out to you, what emotions you experienced, and any insights God has revealed to you. Feel free to write a personal prayer, expressing your thoughts, gratitude, or requests for healing.

Reflection & Journaling

Journaling Prompt:

What stood out to you most in this chapter?

_____

_____

_____

_____

_____

Take a moment and write a prayer to God and ask him to help you with healing these emotions.

_____

_____

_____

_____

_____

Notes & Reflections:

(Use this space to write thoughts or anything on your heart.)

_____

_____

_____

_____

_____

_____

_____

_____

_____

_____

_____

_____

_____

_____

_____

_____

_____

_____

Prayer Space:

Write a personal prayer for this season of your life. Ask God for wisdom, healing, or strength to continue your journey.

_____

_____

_____

_____

_____

_____

_____

_____

_____

Spiritual Reset: God's Truth vs. Spiritual Manipulation

Take a moment to pause and recenter. Let this Scripture speak truth and peace over your heart before moving forward.

*Scripture: **John 8:32** "Then you will know the truth, and the truth will set you free."*

Chapter 1 Scripture Summary

Mark 10:42-45: "*Jesus called them together and said, "You know that those who are regarded as rulers of the Gentiles lord it over them, and their high officials exercise authority over them. Not so with you. Instead, whoever wants to become great among you must be your servant, and whoever wants to be first must be slave of all. For even the Son of Man did not come to be served, but to serve, and to give his life as a ransom for many."*

Ephesians 2:8-9: "*For it is by grace you have been saved, through faith—and this is not from yourselves, it is the gift of God—not by works, so that no one can boast."*

Luke 4:18: "*The Spirit of the Lord is on me, because he has anointed me to proclaim good news to the poor. He has sent me to proclaim freedom for the prisoners and recovery of sight for the blind, to set the oppressed free,"*

Matthew 4:1-11: "*Then Jesus was led by the Spirit into the wilderness to be tempted by the devil. After fasting forty days and forty nights, he was hungry. The tempter came to him and said, "If you are the Son of God, tell these stones to become bread."*

Jesus answered, "It is written: 'Man shall not live on bread alone, but on every word that comes from the mouth of God.'"

Then the devil took him to the holy city and had him stand on the highest point of the temple. "If you are the Son of God," he said, "throw yourself down. For it is written:"

"'He will command his angels concerning you, and they will lift you up in their hands, so that you will not strike your foot against a stone.'"

Jesus answered him, "It is also written: 'Do not put the Lord your God to the test.'"

Again, the devil took him to a very high mountain and showed him all the kingdoms of the world and their splendor. "All this I will give you," he said, "if you will bow down and worship me."

Jesus said to him, "Away from me, Satan! For it is written: 'Worship the Lord your God, and serve him only.'"

Then the devil left him, and angels came and attended him."

Proverbs 31:8-9: "*Speak up for those who cannot speak for themselves, for the rights of all who are destitute. Speak up and judge fairly; defend the rights of the poor and needy."*

2 Corinthians 8:20-21: "*We want to avoid any criticism of the way we administer this liberal gift. For we are taking pains to do what is right, not only in the eyes of the Lord but also in the eyes of man."*

Deuteronomy 31:8: "*The Lord himself goes before you and will be with you; he will never leave you nor forsake you. Do not be afraid; do not be discouraged.*"

Genesis 50:20: "*You intended to harm me, but God intended it for good to accomplish what is now being done, the saving of many lives.*"

Psalm 147:3: "*He heals the brokenhearted and binds up their wounds.*"

Isaiah 41:10: "*So do not fear, for I am with you; do not be dismayed, for I am your God. I will strengthen you and help you; I will uphold you with my righteous right hand.*"

John 8:32: *"Then you will know the truth, and the truth will set you free."*

CHAPTER TWO

———————— ◆ ————————

THE EMOTIONAL AND
SPIRITUAL IMPACT OF LEAVING

"COME TO ME, WHO ARE ALL WEARY AND
BURDENED, AND I WILL GIVE YOU REST."

MATTHEW 11:28

The Emotional and Spiritual Impact of Leaving

Before Leaving: Understanding Church Hurt vs. Toxic Church Culture

Not every painful church experience means you need to leave. As we discussed in Chapter 1, church hurt is something many believers will face at some point—whether it's through misunderstandings, leadership decisions we disagree with, or personal conflicts within the body of Christ. In many cases, these situations can be resolved through honest communication, accountability, and grace **(Matthew 18:15-17, Ephesians 4:2).**

However, a toxic church culture is different. It goes beyond personal hurt and reflects an ongoing pattern of manipulation, control, secrecy, or spiritual abuse—often with no accountability from leadership. Many people do not leave just because they are hurt; they leave because they realize the environment is unhealthy and no changes are being made.

A healthy church allows for questions, transparency, and biblical accountability. A toxic church, however, demands blind loyalty, suppresses concerns, distorts Scripture to maintain control, and fosters fear rather than faith. When a church consistently prioritizes power over people, it is no longer a safe place to grow spiritually. In these situations, staying is not an act of faith—leaving can be an act of obedience to God.

The Emotional and Spiritual Impact of Leaving

Leaving a toxic church isn't just a physical decision—it's an emotional and spiritual journey. You may experience grief, fear, guilt, or even confusion. These feelings are normal, and processing them is key to healing.

But healing isn't about erasing the past—it's about allowing God's grace to bring clarity, healing, and restoration. No matter how painful your experience, God is not done with your story. He is faithful to bring truth, renewal, and a deeper relationship with Him.

In this chapter, we'll explore:

- **The emotional and spiritual struggles that come with leaving.**
- **How to process grief, fear, and guilt in a healthy, biblical way.**
- **Holding onto God's truth as you move forward.**

You don't have to walk this journey alone. Jesus is your healer, your foundation, and your guide. There is freedom on the other side of faith-related pain.

Common Emotional Responses:

Emotion	Thoughts & Feelings
Guilt	"Am I betraying God, my church or my friends by leaving?"
Fear	"Will I lose my faith, friends or my relationship with God?"
Grief	"I feel like I'm mourning the loss of a community."
Confusion	"I knew something wasn't right, but I didn't know what."

Identifying Your Own Emotions

Everyone processes emotions differently. Maybe you're feeling something we haven't listed—like anger, relief or loneliness. Use the space below to name what you're feeling in your own words, and write out the thoughts or questions that come with it.

God can handle your emotions—whatever they are. Honesty is the beginning of healing.

Emotion	Thoughts & Feelings

Moving Forward

Once you've named what you're feeling, take a breath. This isn't the end of your story—it's a moment of clarity. You don't have to stay stuck here. On the next page, we'll walk through practical steps to begin working through the common emotions people may experience—so you can move forward in healing, hope, and truth.

Steps Toward Healing:

1. **Acknowledge Your Feelings** – Accepting and processing your emotions is the first step toward healing.
2. **Find Support** – Surround yourself with people who validate your experience and provide emotional and spiritual encouragement.
3. **Rebuild Your Faith** – Take time to redefine your personal relationship with God outside of a toxic environment.
4. **Set Boundaries** – Create emotional and physical distance from the toxic church and its influence.
5. **Give Yourself Time**– Healing is a journey; allow yourself to heal at your own pace.

Steps Toward Healing: In Action

1. Acknowledge Your Feelings

It's okay to grieve. It's okay to feel angry. **Jesus Himself** experienced righteous anger toward religious leaders who misrepresented **God (Matthew 23:13-36)**. Ignoring your emotions won't make them go away—**allow yourself to feel them, process them, and bring them before God.**

- You may experience **grief, betrayal, fear, or confusion.** All of these emotions are valid.
- Suppressing your feelings won't lead to healing—**surrendering them to Jesus will.**
- **Talk to God openly** about how you feel. He welcomes your honesty—then **lay them down at His feet.**

2. Find Support

You were never meant to carry this alone. **Healing happens in community**, and there are people who will **walk with you through this.**

Galatians 6:2 *"Carry each other's burdens, and in this way you will fulfill the law of Christ."*

- **Find safe people** who validate your experience—a trusted **Christian** friend, a mentor, or a faith-based support group. Make sure these people have your relationship with God a top priority.
- **Seek counseling** a **Christian counselor** who understands religious trauma can be a valuable guide.
- **Distance yourself from voices** that dismiss your pain or pressure you to return to an unhealthy environment.

3. Rebuild Your Faith in Christ, Not a Church

It's easy to associate faith with **a church, a pastor, or a specific community.** But **your faith should be anchored in Jesus, not in people.**

Matthew 7:24-25 *"Therefore everyone who hears these words of mine and puts them into practice is like a wise man who built his house on the rock. The rain came down, the streams rose, and the winds blew and beat against that house; yet it did not fall, because it had its foundation on the rock."*

- **Read the Bible for yourself**—let **God's Word** speak truth over your experience.
- Take time to explore **who God is apart from the church environment you left.**
- Trust that **Jesus is still your foundation,** even if your church experience was **shaken.**

4. Set Healthy Boundaries

Walking away from a toxic church **doesn't mean you have to engage in every conversation about it.** It's okay to **protect your peace** by setting boundaries.

Proverbs 4:23 *"Above all else, guard your heart, for everything you do flows from it."*

- **Unfollow social media pages** or leaders that stir **anxiety, guilt, or shame.**
- **Be selective about who you allow** to speak into your spiritual journey.
- **If people from your former church** pressure you or attempt to manipulate you, know that **you do not owe them an explanation.**

5. Give Yourself Grace & Time

Healing **isn't a straight path**—it's a journey. **Some days you'll feel strong, and other days you may question everything.** That's okay. **Jesus is patient with you, so be patient with yourself.**

Ecclesiastes 3:1,3 *"There is a time for everything... a time to heal, a time to build up."*

- **Don't compare your healing process** to someone else's.
- Give yourself **permission to rest, process, and take small steps forward.**
- Trust that **God is working in you, even when you don't see it.**

My Personal Experience: When Church Didn't Feel Right...

For me, attending this church wasn't just about finding a place of worship—it was about my career. I was there for an internship and what I believed was a step toward a career in full-time ministry. I had envisioned a future of serving God, helping others grow in their faith. But over time, I started to notice something unsettling. This church functioned more like a corporation than a Christ-centered community. It was often referred to as "the organization", and that was exactly how it felt—structured, performance-driven, and business-oriented, rather than a Spirit-led body of believers.

I recognized the red flags because I had experienced a healthy church before. I knew what it looked like when a church truly operated under the leadership of Christ. But I also knew that for many people, this was their only church experience. If you've never seen anything different, how do you know something is wrong? That's what makes spiritual manipulation so dangerous—it distorts what faith is supposed to be.

There were moments when I wrestled with fear and doubt. Am I being too critical? Am I dishonoring God by questioning leadership? But deep down, I couldn't ignore one pressing thought: If Jesus were here, would He be flipping tables?

That thought reminded me of when Jesus entered the temple and saw that it had become something it was never meant to be—a marketplace rather than a house of worship. His response was righteous anger:

> *"Jesus entered the temple courts and drove out all who were buying and selling there. He overturned the tables of the money changers and the benches of those selling doves. 'It is written,' he said to them, 'My house will be called a house of prayer, but you are making it a den of robbers."* **Matthew 21:12-13**

Jesus wasn't just reacting emotionally—He was defending the holiness of God's house. That passage gave me peace, knowing that sometimes, God calls us to stand against what is wrong, even within His own church.

Through this experience, I learned that following God's will doesn't always mean staying where it's comfortable. Sometimes, He calls us to step into the unknown, trusting Him even when the path is uncertain. Like Esther, who was placed in a position where she had to stand for truth at great personal risk, we, too, may find ourselves in situations where obedience to God requires courage.

Esther didn't know how things would turn out when she approached the king, but she trusted that God had placed her there f*or such a time as this.* **(Esther 4:14)** In the same way, leaving an unhealthy church can feel like stepping into the unknown, but sometimes, God calls us to take that step to defend our faith and uphold His truth. And while I didn't have all the answers at the time, I found peace in knowing that God was not leading me away from something—but toward something greater. He is faithful, and when we trust Him, we will find healing, restoration, and a deeper relationship with Him on the other side.

Moving Forward in Faith

Leaving a toxic church is not just about walking away from something unhealthy—it's about stepping toward Jesus in a new and deeper way. While the pain is real, so is God's faithfulness. What feels like loss now will one day be a testimony of His restoration.

Maybe right now, you feel lost, uncertain, or even angry. Maybe you're grieving the community you once trusted. But hear this: Jesus sees you, He understands your pain, and He is not finished with you yet.

This chapter of your life is not the end of your faith story—it's a turning point. God is leading you somewhere new, somewhere better, somewhere He intended all along.

Take a moment to breathe, to pray, and to sit with Him. The same Jesus who overturned tables in the temple is now clearing the way for you to step into the freedom and healing He has for you.

You may have left a church, but you have not left Jesus. And He has never left you.

Biblical Encouragement:

Psalm 62:1-2 *"Truly my soul finds rest in God; my salvation comes from Him. Truly He is my rock and my salvation; He is my fortress, I will never be shaken."*

2 Timothy 1:7 *"For God has not given us a spirit of fear, but of power and of love and of a sound mind."*

Psalm 34:18 *"The Lord is close to the brokenhearted and saves those who are crushed in spirit."*

What's Next?

Leaving a toxic church is a life-altering decision—one that carries emotional weight, spiritual doubts, and personal struggles. But recognizing the problem is only the first step.

Now, it's time to take action.

In the next chapter, we'll walk through practical steps to help you leave well—from seeking God's wisdom and wise counsel to creating an exit plan and setting boundaries. Leaving won't be easy, and opposition may come, but you don't have to walk this path alone. God is with you, and on the other side of obedience is freedom.

Journaling Exercise: Processing Your Emotions

1. Write a letter to your past self when you were still in the toxic church. What would you say to encourage and protect yourself?

Answer: _____

_____

_____

_____

2. What emotions have been the strongest since leaving (fear, guilt, relief, anger, grief) and why?

Answer: _____

_____

_____

_____

3. Looking back, do you see God moving and how do you see him now?

Answer: _____

_____

_____

_____

Prayer for Emotional Healing

Jesus, I bring my pain and burdens to You. I release my fear and guilt, knowing that You are leading me to peace. Heal my heart and restore my faith in Your love. Amen.

Journaling & Prayer Reflection

At the end of each chapter, take a moment to pause and reflect. Use this space to write down what stood out to you, what emotions you experienced, and any insights God has revealed to you. Feel free to write a personal prayer, expressing your thoughts, gratitude, or requests for healing.

Reflection & Journaling

Journaling Prompt:

Which of the Five steps are you on and which one is the hardest for you to move through?

_____

_____

_____

_____

_____

Write about your experience at church and what does not feel right to you.

_____

_____

_____

_____

_____

Notes & Reflections:

(Use this space to write thoughts or anything on your heart.)

_____

_____

_____

_____

_____

_____

_____

_____

_____

_____

_____

_____

_____

_____

_____

_____

_____

_____

Prayer Space

Write a personal prayer for this season of your life. Ask God for wisdom, healing, or strength to continue your journey.

_____

_____

_____

_____

_____

_____

_____

_____

_____

_____

Spiritual Reset: Finding Peace After Spiritual Hurt

Take a moment to pause and recenter. Let this Scripture speak truth and peace over your heart before moving forward.

Scripture: **Matthew 11:28** *"Come to me, all you who are weary and burdened, and I will give you rest."*

Chapter 2 Scripture Summary

Matthew 18:15-17: *"If your brother or sister sins, go and point out their fault, just between the two of you. If they listen to you, you have won them over. But if they will not listen, take one or two others along, so that 'every matter may be established by the testimony of two or three witnesses.' If they still refuse to listen, tell it to the church; and if they refuse to listen even to the church, treat them as you would a pagan or a tax collector."*

Ephesians 4:2: *"Be completely humble and gentle; be patient, bearing with one another in love."*

1 Corinthians 3:10-11: *"By the grace God has given me, I laid a foundation as a wise builder, and someone else is building on it. But each one should build with care. For no one can lay any foundation other than the one already laid, which is Jesus Christ."*

Psalm 62:1-2: *"Truly my soul finds rest in God; my salvation comes from him. Truly he is my rock and my salvation; he is my fortress, I will never be shaken."*

2 Timothy 1:7: *"For the Spirit God gave us does not make us timid, but gives us power, love and self-discipline."*

Psalm 34:18: *"The Lord is close to the brokenhearted and saves those who are crushed in spirit."*

Matthew 11:28: *"Come to me, all you who are weary and burdened, and I will give you rest."*

Galatians 6:2: *"Share each other's burdens, and in this way obey the law of Christ."*

Matthew 7:24-25: *"Anyone who listens to my teaching and follows it is wise, like a person who builds a house on solid rock. Though the rain comes in torrents and the floodwaters rise and the winds beat against that house, it won't collapse because it is built on bedrock."*

Proverbs 4:23: *"Guard your heart above all else, for it determines the course of your life."*

Ecclesiastes 3:1,3: *"For everything there is a season, a time for every activity under heaven... A time to kill and a time to heal. A time to tear down and a time to build up."*

Matthew 21:12-13: *"Jesus entered the Temple and began to drive out all the people buying and selling animals for sacrifice. He knocked over the tables of the money changers and the chairs of those selling doves. He said to them, 'The Scriptures declare, My Temple will be called a house of prayer,' but you have turned it into a den of thieves!"*

Esther 4:14: *"If you keep quiet at a time like this, deliverance and relief for the Jews will arise from some other place, but you and your relatives will die. Who knows if perhaps you were made queen for just such a time as this?"*

CHAPTER THREE

———————— ◆ ————————

STEPS TO LEAVING AN
UNHEALTHY CHURCH

"I WILL INSTRUCT YOU AND TEACH YOU IN
THE WAY YOU SHOULD GO; I WILL COUNSEL
YOU WITH MY LOVING EYE ON YOU."

PSALM 32:8

Steps to Leaving an Unhealthy Church

Once you recognize that your experience was beyond church hurt and that you have been part of an unhealthy, toxic church culture, the next step is deciding how to leave—a decision that requires wisdom and courage.

Leaving a toxic church is not just about walking away; it's about walking toward healing, truth, and the freedom God desires for you. Jesus never intended for His followers to be bound by fear, guilt, or manipulation. Instead, He calls us into a relationship rooted in grace, truth, and spiritual growth.

In this chapter, we'll discuss how to leave well, navigate potential challenges, and take steps toward spiritual and emotional healing as you move forward in faith.

Practical Steps for Leaving:

Pray for Wisdom	Ask God for discernment in your decision
Seek Wise Counsel	Find trusted friends, mentors, or counselors who understand church toxicity.
Educate Yourself	Read about spiritual abuse and religious trauma to affirm your experience and clarify your next steps.
Create an Exit Plan	Consider how and when you will leave, and whether you need to have a conversation with leadership.
Prepare for Opposition	Toxic churches often discourage leaving; be ready to stand firm in your decision.
Set Boundaries	Be prepared for resistance from church leaders or members and know how to respond.
Allow yourself to Grieve	Understand that leaving a church is a loss and give yourself time to process.

Practical Steps for Leaving: In Action

1. Pray for Wisdom

Before making any major decision, **seek God first (James 1:5)**. Ask for clarity, peace, and direction. If you're unsure whether leaving is the right choice, **ask God to confirm it in His Word.**

God is not a **God of confusion (1 Corinthians 14:33)**. He will guide you in His perfect timing.

- **Does this church reflect the love, grace, and truth of Jesus?**
- **Is my faith growing here, or am I spiritually stagnant?**
- **Do I feel manipulated or controlled rather than shepherded and discipled?**
- **Have I tried to address the concern/issue with leadership?**
- **If so, was accountability and a resolution provided?**

2. Seek Wise Counsel

Proverbs 11:14 reminds us that **"where there is no guidance, a people falls, but in an abundance of counselors there is safety."** Talk to **trusted believers** who have your best interest at heart. Seek counsel from those who have **a biblical perspective on church health**, not just those who will tell you what you want to hear.

3. Educate Yourself

If you've been in a toxic church for a long time, you may struggle with **trusting your own judgment**. Educating yourself on **spiritual abuse, religious trauma, and healthy church leadership** will help you see the situation more clearly. Scripture warns us about **false teachers and spiritual wolves (Matthew 7:15-20)**, and it's important to recognize when those warnings apply.

4. Create an Exit Plan

Leaving impulsively might feel right in the moment, but **a well-thought-out plan will help you transition smoothly**. Every situation is different. **Some people can leave quietly, while others may need to address leadership or friends before stepping away.**

Ask yourself:

- Do I need to have a conversation with leadership, or will that cause unnecessary harm?
- How will I respond if they try to manipulate or guilt-trip me into staying?
- Do I need to inform anyone close to me about my departure?

Possible responses:

- **This is the right decision for me.**
- **I hear you, but I have already made up my mind.**
- **Thank you for your concern, but it is best for me to leave.**

5. Prepare for Opposition

Not everyone will understand or support your decision but remember this: **God is not a church building. Your relationship with Him is not dependent on where you worship.** Do not let fear keep you in a spiritually harmful place.

Toxic Churches often:

- Accuse people of "backsliding" or "rebelling" when they leave.
- Use **fear tactics** to make people believe they are abandoning God.
- Cut off relationships with those who leave.

6. Set Boundaries

If leaving your church means closing the chapter on certain relationships, **that's okay. Not everyone has access to your spiritual journey.** Boundaries are not **unchristian**—they are **wise**. Jesus Himself set boundaries when people tried to misuse His ministry

"But Jesus often withdrew to lonely places and prayed." **Luke 5:16**

Decide in advance:

- **Will I respond if the pastor or leadership reaches out?**
- **Am I comfortable explaining my decision, or do I need to distance myself?**
- **Do I need to unfollow social media pages that are emotionally triggering?**

7. Find Support

Healing happens **in healthy communities**. Leaving a toxic church can feel isolating, so surround yourself with **believers who will encourage and uplift you**.

This could be:

- A **trusted Christian friend** who understands your situation.
- A **counselor or mentor** who specializes in church trauma.
- A **new church community** where you can **heal and grow in Christ**.

8. Allow Yourself to Grieve

Leaving a church can feel like losing **a family, a home, and even a piece of your identity**. Jesus understands **your grief and betrayal**. He, too, was rejected by religious leaders, misunderstood, and abandoned by those closest to Him **(John 1:11, Matthew 26:56). He is with you in this process.**

Give yourself permission to:

- Mourn the relationships you're leaving behind.
- Acknowledge the disappointment of being hurt by the church.
- Release the expectations you once had for that community.
- Maintain friendships with those still tied to the church if safe and desired.

Leaving with a Godly Heart Posture:

Leaving well means departing with grace, love, and a focus on Christ. **Romans 12:18** says, *"If it is possible, as far as it depends on you, live at peace with everyone."* **Ephesians 4:31-32** urges believers to *"Get rid of all bitterness, rage, and anger... Be kind and compassionate to one another, forgiving each other, just as in Christ God forgave you."* Seek healing, protect your heart, and trust God to lead you into a healthier faith community.

Biblical Encouragement:

Psalm 37:23-24 *"The Lord makes firm the steps of the one who delights in Him; though he may stumble, he will not fall, for the Lord upholds him with His hand."*

Psalm 46:1 *"God is our refuge and strength, an ever-present help in trouble."*

Colossians 3:15 *"Let the peace of Christ rule in your hearts. '*

What's Next?

Leaving a **toxic church** may feel **overwhelming**, but **it is not the end of your faith**—it is an opportunity to **rediscover a deeper, more authentic relationship with Jesus.** As you take this step, **God will walk with you**, providing **wisdom, healing, and the assurance that He has something greater ahead.**

Trust in Him. Even when the path feels uncertain, **God's plans are always for your good (Psalm 32:8). He is faithful, He is present, and He will lead you into freedom, renewal, and a deeper understanding of His love.**

In the next chapter, we'll walk through the **practical steps to healing from church hurt**—how to prepare **emotionally, spiritually, and relationally** so you can step into the **next season of your faith with wisdom, grace, and confidence in Christ.**

Journaling Exercise: Creating Your Exit Plan

1. What are your biggest fears about leaving and how can God comfort you in those fears?

Answer: _____

_____

_____

_____

2. Who are safe people you can talk to about your decision?

Answer: _____

_____

_____

_____

3. What steps can you take to leave in a way that protects your emotional and spiritual well-being?

Answer: _____

_____

_____

_____

Prayer for Strength & Courage

Father, I feel uncertain, but I know You are guiding me. Give me the strength to walk away from what is unhealthy and trust You for what's ahead. Amen.

Practical Checklists for Key Steps

These checklists are designed to help you take practical steps toward healing and growth. Use them as a guide to track your progress and stay intentional about your journey.

Checklist: Preparing to Leave a Toxic Church

✔ Pray for wisdom and discernment ☐

✔ Seek wise counsel from trusted mentors ☐

✔ Create an exit plan (timeline, steps, next church options, etc.) ☐

✔ Prepare for opposition (set boundaries, have responses ready) ☐

✔ Surround yourself with a strong support system ☐

✔ Allow yourself to grieve and process emotions ☐

Journaling & Prayer Reflection

At the end of each chapter, take a moment to pause and reflect. Use this space to write down what stood out to you, what emotions you experienced, and any insights God has revealed to you. Feel free to write a personal prayer, expressing your thoughts, gratitude, or requests for healing.

Reflection & Journaling
Journaling Prompt:

Which one of these practical steps towards leaving are you on? Which one do you find the most difficult and why?

_____

_____

_____

_____

_____

Write about your personal experience of leaving or your personal experience wrestling to leave.

_____

_____

_____

_____

_____

Notes & Reflections:

(Use this space to write thoughts or anything on your heart.)

_____

_____

_____

_____

_____

_____

_____

_____

_____

_____

_____

_____

_____

_____

_____

_____

_____

_____

Prayer Space

Write a personal prayer for this season of your life. Ask God for wisdom, healing, or strength to continue your journey.

_____

_____

_____

_____

_____

_____

_____

_____

_____

Spiritual Reset: God Goes Before You

Take a moment to pause and recenter. Let this Scripture speak truth and peace over your heart before moving forward.

Scripture: **Isaiah 43:2** *"When you pass through the waters, I will be with you; and when you pass through the rivers, they will not sweep over you. When you walk through the fire, you will not be burned; the flames will not set you ablaze."*

Chapter 3 Scripture Summary

James 1:5: "*If any of you lacks wisdom, you should ask God, who gives generously to all without finding fault, and it will be given to you.*"

1 Corinthians 14:33: "*For God is not a God of disorder but of peace—as in all the congregations of the Lord's people.*"

Proverbs 11:14: "*For lack of guidance a nation falls, but victory is won through many advisers.*"

Matthew 7:15-20: "*Watch out for false prophets. They come to you in sheep's clothing, but inwardly they are ferocious wolves. By their fruit you will recognize them. Do people pick grapes from thornbushes, or figs from thistles? Likewise, every good tree bears good fruit, but a bad tree bears bad fruit. A good tree cannot bear bad fruit, and a bad tree cannot bear good fruit. Every tree that does not bear good fruit is cut down and thrown into the fire. Thus, by their fruit you will recognize them.*"

Romans 12:18: "*If it is possible, as far as it depends on you, live at peace with everyone.*"

Ephesians 4:31-32: "*Get rid of all bitterness, rage and anger, brawling and slander, along with every form of malice. Be kind and compassionate to one another, forgiving each other, just as in Christ God forgave you.*"

Psalm 37:23-24: "*The Lord makes firm the steps of the one who delights in him; though he may stumble, he will not fall, for the Lord upholds him with his hand.*"

Psalm 46:1: "*God is our refuge and strength, an ever-present help in trouble.*"

Colossians 3:15: "*Let the peace of Christ rule in your hearts, since as members of one body you were called to peace. And be thankful.*"

Isaiah 43:2: "*When you pass through the waters, I will be with you; and when you pass through the rivers, they will not sweep over you. When you walk through the fire, you will not be burned; the flames will not set you ablaze.*"

Luke 5:16: "*But Jesus often withdrew to lonely places and prayed.*"

John 1:11: "*He came to that which was his own, but his own did not receive him.*"

Matthew 26:56: "*Then all the disciples deserted him and fled.*"

Psalm 32:8: "*I will instruct you and teach you in the way you should go; I will counsel you with my loving eye on you.*"

CHAPTER FOUR

—————— ✦ ——————

HEALING CHURCH WOUNDS

"HE HEALS THE BROKENHEARTED AND
BINDS UP THEIR WOUNDS."

PSALM 147:3

Healing Church Wounds

Now that you've recognized your church was toxic and made the decision to leave, what comes next? How do you process the hurt, the confusion, and the loss? Walking away was a necessary step, but now it's time to heal and step into the freedom Christ has for you.

Healing isn't instant. It's a journey, and it looks different for everyone. Some find peace quickly, while others wrestle with deep wounds for a long time. Both are okay. Your healing is between you and God—it doesn't have to look like anyone else's.

One of the enemy's most subtle traps is comparison—making you feel like your healing should look like someone else's timeline. It minimizes your pain and pressures you to 'move on' before you're ready. But healing isn't linear, and it doesn't come with a deadline. God is healing you in His perfect timing, not anyone else's

2 Corinthians 3:17 reminds us:
"Now the Lord is the Spirit, and where the Spirit of the Lord is, there is freedom."

In this chapter, we'll explore what it looks like to heal from spiritual wounds, rebuild trust, and walk in true freedom. No matter where you are in the process, know this: healing is a journey and God will walk with you through it all!

Forgiveness & Reconciliation: Do I Need to Forgive?

Healing from church trauma does not mean you have to **reconcile** with the people who harmed you. Forgiveness does not require reconciliation.

Forgiveness is about freeing yourself from bitterness, surrendering the pain to God, and allowing Him to bring healing.

Reconciliation requires accountability and change. If the toxic church or individuals refuse to acknowledge wrongdoing, reconciliation may not be possible—and that's okay. Boundaries are biblical. You can forgive someone and still maintain distance. Jesus forgave, but He also set boundaries

Examples of Jesus setting boundaries:

In **Matthew 21:23-27** and **22:15-22**, Jesus refused to allow religious leaders to trap him with questions designed to make him look foolish, instead, he interacted with them using courage and wisdom, calling them out on their motives.

"Jesus entered the temple courts, and, while he was teaching, the chief priests and the elders of the people came to him. "By what authority are you doing these things?" they asked. "And who gave you this authority?"

Jesus replied, "I will also ask you one question. If you answer me, I will tell you by what authority I am doing these things. John's baptism—where did it come from? Was it from heaven, or of human origin?"

"They discussed it among themselves and said, "If we say, 'From heaven,' he will ask, 'Then why didn't you believe him?' But if we say, 'Of human origin'—we are afraid of the people, for they all hold that John was a prophet."

"So they answered Jesus, "We don't know." Then he said, "Neither will I tell you by what authority I am doing these things." **Matthew 21:23-27**

"Then the Pharisees went out and laid plans to trap him in his words. They sent their disciples to him along with the Herodians. "Teacher," they said, "we know that you are a man of integrity and that you teach the way of God in accordance with the truth. You aren't swayed by others, because you pay no attention to who they are. Tell us then, what is your opinion? Is it right to pay the imperial tax[a] to Caesar or not?"

"But Jesus, knowing their evil intent, said, "You hypocrites, why are you trying to trap me? Show me the coin used for paying the tax." They brought him a denarius, and he asked them, "Whose image is this? And whose inscription?" "Caesar's," they replied. Then he said to them, "So give back to Caesar what is Caesar's, and to God what is God's." When they heard this, they were amazed. So they left him and went away." **Matthew 22:15-22**

Forgiveness is for your spiritual freedom—it's not a pass for abuse or an invitation to return to a toxic environment. Jesus never called us to stay in places that harm us.

"As Jesus said to his disciples, "If the home is worthy, let your peace rest on it; but if it is not, let your peace return to you. And if anyone will not receive you or listen to your words, leave that home and shake the dust off your feet." **Matthew 10:13-14**

Steps to Healing:

Step	Description
Allow Yourself to Grieve	Recognize that leaving a church is a loss, and it's okay to mourn.
Separate God from the Institution	Your faith is not dependent on a single church or leader.
Rebuild Trust	Find safe spaces where you can share your story and receive encouragement.
Rediscover a Personal Connection with Jesus	Focus on spiritual practices that bring you peace and healing.
Engage in Christian Counseling	If needed, seek professional help to process church trauma.
Surround Yourself with Healthy Community	Find people who support your healing journey.
Develop New Spiritual Practices	Explore prayer, worship, and biblical studies.

Practical Steps to Healing: In Action

The journey to healing is deeply personal, but **God is faithful to restore what has been broken.** Healing isn't about erasing the past—it's about allowing **God's grace** to shape your future. Here are some steps that can help you process your experience and move forward in **freedom through Christ:**

1. Allow Yourself to Grieve

Leaving a church, no matter how unhealthy, is still a loss. You may feel like you're mourning **a community, a purpose, or even a version of faith you once knew. It's okay to grieve.**

John 11:35 *"Jesus wept."*

- **Grieving is part of healing.** Don't rush the process.
- **Acknowledge your emotions, but don't let them define you.**
- **Bring your grief to Jesus, who binds up the brokenhearted (Isaiah 61:1).**
- **Let yourself feel, but don't let pain become your identity.** Your past may shape you, but it does not define your future.

2. Separate God from the Institution

One of the biggest challenges after leaving a toxic church is **untangling your faith from the institution.** If spiritual leaders misrepresented **Jesus**, it can make you question everything.

- **Your faith is not dependent on a single church or leader.**
- **God is not the pastor who manipulated you.**
- **Jesus is still Jesus, even if people misused His name.**

Romans 8:39 *"Nothing in all creation will be able to separate us from the love of God that is in Christ Jesus our Lord."*

- **God is bigger than a church building—He is unshaken by human failures.**
- **God still desires a personal relationship with you, even if your relationship with the church is broken.**

3. Trusting God First

After being hurt, it may feel impossible to trust again. But **Scripture** calls us to place our ultimate **trust in God alone.** People will always have the capacity to disappoint, but **God is faithful** and **unchanging.**

Proverbs 3:5-6 *"Trust in the Lord with all your heart and lean not on your own understanding; in all your ways submit to Him, and He will make your paths straight."*

- **When we trust Him first, God gives wisdom to test all things by His Word.**
- **Leaders are human and will fail, but God never does—He remains faithful.**
- **True healing grows in Christ-centered spaces grounded in God's Word, His grace, and His truth.**

4. Rediscover a Personal Relationship with Jesus

In toxic church environments, **faith often feels controlled or dictated by leadership.** Now that you're free from that, it's time to **rebuild your personal relationship with Jesus.**

John 14:27 *"Peace I leave with you; my peace I give you. I do not give to you as the world gives. Do not let your hearts be troubled and do not be afraid."*

- **Jesus desires relationship, not religious obligation.**
- **Spend time in prayer, not out of duty—but out of desire.**
- **Read God's Word for yourself and let Him speak directly to you.**
- **Worship without the pressure of performance—let it be personal.**

Freedom in Christ means rediscovering faith in a way that brings healing, not fear.

5. Engage in Christian Counseling (if you feel stuck)

Religious trauma is real. If you find yourself struggling with **deep wounds, anxiety, or spiritual confusion,** seeking professional help **is a sign of wisdom, not weakness.**

Proverbs 15:22 *"Plans fail for lack of counsel, but with many advisers they succeed."*

- **Healing takes time, and God works through wise counsel.**
- **A Christian counselor can help you process spiritual abuse in a biblical way.**
- **There is no shame in needing support—God designed us for healing through others.**

6. Surround Yourself with Healthy Community

One of the most difficult yet necessary steps is finding a **healthy, Christ-centered community** where you can grow.

Hebrews 10:25 *"Do not give up meeting together, as some are in the habit of doing, but encourage one another."*

- **You were never meant to walk this journey alone.**
- **Seek relationships that encourage growth, not control.**
- **Take your time—God will bring the right people into your life.**

7. Rebuilding Your Spiritual Practices

After leaving a toxic church, staying rooted in **God's Word** and maintaining a strong relationship with **Him** is essential. However, some may find that reading the Bible or engaging in prayer feels difficult due to past experiences. If this is you, don't give up—**God's Word** is still your foundation. If prayer feels hard, start small. Just talk to God like a friend. If reading the Bible feels overwhelming, begin with comforting passages like **Psalms** or **Jesus' words in the Gospels.**

2 Timothy 3:16-17 *"All Scripture is God-breathed and is useful for teaching, rebuking, correcting, and training in righteousness, so that the servant of God may be thoroughly equipped for every good work."*

- **Lean into Scripture—God's Word is alive and active (Hebrews 4:12) and will always bring truth, healing, and renewal.**
- **Draw near to Him through prayer—Even if it feels hard at first, God hears every word, and He meets you where you are.**
- **Let go of legalistic habits and embrace a faith built on grace, not fear.**

Replacing Lies with Truth

Healing isn't just about leaving what was harmful—it's about renewing your heart and mind with what is true. One of the subtle wounds left by toxic church culture is the way it distorts God's voice. Maybe you were told things that made you feel ashamed, weak, rebellious, or unworthy. These lies often linger long after we leave.

But here's the good news: God's Word offers something better. His truth heals, restores, and sets us free. On the next page, you'll find a chart of common lies people wrestle with after spiritual abuse or church hurt—paired with biblical truths to help you renew your mind and move forward in freedom.

These Scriptures are already explored throughout this chapter, so you can revisit them with fresh perspective and confidence.

Truths to Replace Lies:

Lie	Truth	Scripture
"You're walking away from God."	God is still with me. He brings freedom, not fear.	2 Corinthians 3:17
"You're not allowed to grieve."	Jesus grieved too, my pain matters.	John 11:35
"You're just being rebellious."	God leads me to truth and healing, not control.	Isaiah 61:1
"Your faith is broken."	God is restoring and renewing my faith.	Philippians 1:6
"You'll never find a place to belong."	God still has a purpose and a future for me.	Jeremiah 29:11

Reflection:

Have you ever believed any of these lies?

_____

_____

_____

_____

_____

Lies vs. Truth: Your Turn

Take a moment to reflect on any lies you've believed about yourself, your faith, or your worth because of your church experience. In the table below, write out:

- **The lie you've wrestled with**
- **The truth God wants to speak over it**
- **A Scripture that affirms that truth**

Use this as a tool to renew your mind and stand firm in God's promises.

Truths to Replace Lies:

Lies I believed	Truth from God's Word	Supporting Scripture

Reflection:

Spend time in prayer, asking God to help you fully believe the truth He's spoken over your life.

_____

_____

_____

_____

_____

Healing is a Journey- Not a Race

Your faith is **not broken—God is renewing and strengthening it.** Stay in **His Word**, remain connected to **Him**, and trust that **He** is leading you forward.

Healing looks different for everyone. Some will move forward **quickly**, while others will take **years** to process what happened and **that's okay!**

What matters most is that you are walking toward Jesus.

God is not rushing you.
God is not disappointed in you.
God is simply inviting you to keep moving forward—one step at a time.

Philippians 1:6 reminds us:
"He who began a good work in you will carry it on to completion until the day of Christ Jesus."

You are healing.
You are growing.
And Jesus is right there with you.

What's Next?

Now that we've explored **healing**, the next step is stepping into **a healthy, Christ-centered church community**—one that nurtures your faith, encourages spiritual growth, and reflects **God's design for His church.**

In the next chapter, we'll explore:

- **Why church community is important**
- **What to look for in a church that reflects Christ**
- **Practical steps to finding a new church home**

Biblical Encouragement:

Isaiah 61:1 "The Spirit of the Sovereign Lord is on me, because the Lord has anointed me to proclaim good news to the poor. He has sent me to bind up the brokenhearted, to proclaim freedom for the captives and release from darkness for the prisoners."

Jeremiah 29:11 "For I know the plans I have for you, declares the Lord, plans to prosper you and not to harm you, plans to give you a hope and a future."

Joel 2:25 "I will restore to you the years that the swarming locust has eaten."

Journaling Exercise: Steps Toward Healing

1. What are three things you need to heal from?

Answer: _____

_____

_____

_____

2. What boundaries do you need to set with past church members or leaders?

Answer: _____

_____

_____

_____

3. What are some small but meaningful ways you can reconnect with God on your own terms?

Answer: _____

_____

_____

_____

Prayer for Restoration

Lord, I surrender my pain to You. Heal my wounds and show me what it means to experience Your love apart from fear and control. Restore my faith in Your goodness. Amen.

Practical Checklists for Key Steps

These checklists are designed to help you take practical steps toward healing and growth. Use them as a guide to track your progress and stay intentional about your journey.

Checklist: Steps Toward Healing

✔ Acknowledge and process your emotions honestly ☐

✔ Seek biblical counseling or a trusted support system ☐

✔ Give yourself permission to grieve without guilt ☐

✔ Separate your faith in God from the actions of people ☐

✔ Surround yourself with people who encourage your growth ☐

✔ Rebuild your faith at your own pace, without pressure ☐

Journaling & Prayer Reflection

At the end of each chapter, take a moment to pause and reflect. Use this space to write down what stood out to you, what emotions you experienced, and any insights God has revealed to you. Feel free to write a personal prayer, expressing your thoughts, gratitude, or requests for healing.

Reflection & Journaling

Journaling Prompt:

What step are you on and which one do you find the most challenging? Why?

_____

_____

_____

_____

_____

Write about that experience and what emotions it brought up.

_____

_____

_____

_____

_____

Notes & Reflections:

(Use this space to write thoughts or anything on your heart.)

_____

_____

_____

_____

_____

_____

_____

_____

_____

_____

_____

_____

_____

_____

_____

_____

_____

Prayer Space

Write a personal prayer for this season of your life. Ask God for wisdom, healing, or strength to continue your journey.

_____

_____

_____

_____

_____

_____

_____

_____

_____

_____

Spiritual Reset: God Heals Broken Hearts

Take a moment to pause and recenter. Let this Scripture speak truth and peace over your heart before moving forward.

Scripture: **Psalm 147:3** *"He heals the brokenhearted and binds up their wounds."*

Chapter 4 Scripture Summary

2 Corinthians 3:17: "*Now the Lord is the Spirit, and where the Spirit of the Lord is, there is freedom.*"

Matthew 10:13-14: "*If the home is deserving, let your peace rest on it; if it is not, let your peace return to you. If anyone will not welcome you or listen to your words, leave that home or town and shake the dust off your feet.*"

Matthew 21:23-27: "*Jesus entered the temple courts, and, while he was teaching, the chief priests and the elders of the people came to him. "By what authority are you doing these things?" they asked. "And who gave you this authority?"*

Jesus replied, "I will also ask you one question. If you answer me, I will tell you by what authority I am doing these things. John's baptism—where did it come from? Was it from heaven, or of human origin?"

They discussed it among themselves and said, "If we say, 'From heaven,' he will ask, 'Then why didn't you believe him?' But if we say, 'Of human origin'—we are afraid of the people, for they all hold that John was a prophet."

So they answered Jesus, "We don't know."

Then he said, "Neither will I tell you by what authority I am doing these things."

Matthew 22:15-22: "*Then the Pharisees went out and laid plans to trap him in his words. They sent their disciples to him along with the Herodians. "Teacher," they said, "we know that you are a man of integrity and that you teach the way of God in accordance with the truth. You aren't swayed by others, because you pay no attention to who they are. Tell us then, what is your opinion? Is it right to pay the imperial tax to Caesar or not?"*

But Jesus, knowing their evil intent, said, "You hypocrites, why are you trying to trap me? Show me the coin used for paying the tax."

They brought him a denarius, and he asked them, "Whose image is this? And whose inscription?"

"Caesar's," they replied.

Then he said to them, "So give back to Caesar what is Caesar's, and to God what is God's."

When they heard this, they were amazed. So they left him and went away.

Isaiah 61:1: "*The Spirit of the Sovereign Lord is on me, because the Lord has anointed me to proclaim good news to the poor. He has sent me to bind up the brokenhearted, to proclaim freedom for the captives and release from darkness for the prisoners.*"

Romans 8:39: "*Neither height nor depth, nor anything else in all creation, will be able to separate us from the love of God that is in Christ Jesus our Lord.*"

Proverbs 3:5-6: "*Trust in the Lord with all your heart and lean not on your own understanding; in all your ways submit to him, and he will make your paths straight.*"

John 14:27: "*Peace I leave with you; my peace I give you. I do not give to you as the world gives. Do not let your hearts be troubled and do not be afraid.*"

Proverbs 15:22: "*Plans fail for lack of counsel, but with many advisers they succeed.*"

Hebrews 10:25: "*Not giving up meeting together, as some are in the habit of doing, but encouraging one another—and all the more as you see the Day approaching.*"

Hebrews 4:12: "*For the word of God is alive and active. Sharper than any double-edged sword, it penetrates even to dividing soul and spirit, joints and marrow; it judges the thoughts and attitudes of the heart.*"

2 Timothy 3:16-17: "*All Scripture is God-breathed and is useful for teaching, rebuking, correcting and training in righteousness, so that the servant of God may be thoroughly equipped for every good work.*"

Philippians 1:6: "*Being confident of this, that he who began a good work in you will carry it on to completion until the day of Christ Jesus.*"

Jeremiah 29:11: "*For I know the plans I have for you,*" declares the Lord, "*plans to prosper you and not to harm you, plans to give you hope and a future.*"

Joel 2:25: "*I will repay you for the years the locusts have eaten—the great locust and the young locust, the other locusts and the locust swarm—my great army that I sent among you.*"

John 11:35: "*Jesus wept.*"

CHAPTER FIVE

———— ◆ ————

FINDING A HEALTHY
CHURCH COMMUNITY

"AND LET US CONSIDER HOW WE MAY SPUR ONE
ANOTHER ON TOWARD LOVE AND GOOD DEEDS,
NOT GIVING UP MEETING TOGETHER, AS SOME
ARE IN THE HABIT OF DOING, BUT ENCOURAGING
ONE ANOTHER-AND ALL OF THE MORE AS YOU
SEE THE DAY APPROACHING.'

HEBREWS 10:24-25

Finding a Healthy Church Community

After experiencing an unhealthy church, you might wonder if you'll ever feel safe in a church again. Maybe the thought of walking into another congregation brings anxiety, skepticism, or even pain. Is it worth trying again? Can the church still be a place of healing rather than hurt? These are valid questions, and you are not alone in asking them.

It's understandable to feel hesitant, but isolation isn't the answer. The Bible emphasizes the value of gathering with other believers—not just as a routine, but as a vital part of spiritual growth and encouragement. **Acts 2:42** reminds us:

"They devoted themselves to the apostles' teaching and to fellowship, to the breaking of bread and to prayer."

Similarly, **Ecclesiastes 4:9-10** tells us:

"Two are better than one… if either of them falls down, one can help the other up."

Christianity was never meant to be a solo journey. God designed His church to be a place where believers encourage one another, hold each other accountable, and grow together in faith. A healthy church community is not about control, manipulation, or legalism—it's about walking alongside one another in truth and love.

If you're hesitant to return, know this: healing doesn't mean rushing back before you're ready. It means trusting that, in time, God will lead you to a Christ-centered, healthy community where you can thrive.

In this chapter, we'll explore what a healthy church looks like, why community is essential to your healing, and how to take steps toward finding a church that nurtures your faith rather than harms it.

Green Flags of a Healthy Church

Just as it's important to recognize warning signs, it's equally important to know what *healthy* church culture looks like. When you've been hurt by a faith community, it can be difficult to know what "healthy" truly is. In the aftermath of spiritual harm, confusion often lingers—especially when dysfunction was disguised as devotion.

That's where *green flags* come in.

While red flags help us identify what to avoid, green flags offer hope. They remind us that there *are* Christ-centered communities led by humble, Spirit-filled believers who care more about people than performance. These churches may not be perfect—but they are prayerful, accountable, and aligned with the heart of Jesus.

These are the signs of a grace-filled, spiritually nourishing environment—where people are seen, shepherded, and strengthened in Christ. On the following page, you'll find a helpful chart outlining specific traits to look for when seeking a church that supports healing, growth, and transformation. Let it serve as a guide—not just for where to plant yourself next, but for what it truly means to be the Body of Christ.

What to Look for in a Healthy Church:

Green Flag	Description
Servant-Hearted Leadership	Leaders model humility, accountability, and transparency.
Biblical Truth	Scripture is honored, not twisted to manipulate or control.
Healthy Community	People are loved, seen, and accepted without condition.
Grace + Truth Culture	Correction is handled with compassion and clarity.
Encouragement to Grow	Questions are welcomed and spiritual growth is supported.
Financial Transparency	Church finances are handled with integrity and openness.
Safe Discipleship	Spiritual authority is used to equip, not to control.
Mutual Respect	Members and leaders listen, honor, and support each other.
Open Communication	Concerns are heard, not silenced or punished.
Spirit-Led Worship	Worship is Christ-focused, not performance-driven.

Practical Steps to Finding a Healthy Church: In Action

1. Jesus & Biblical Truth

A healthy church is not perfect, but it is anchored in Christ, empowered by the Holy Spirit, and rooted in biblical truth. At the heart of every healthy, Spirit-filled church is Jesus Christ.

Colossians 1:18 *"And He is the head of the body, the church; He is the beginning and the firstborn from among the dead, so that in everything He might have the supremacy."*

- Ask: Is Jesus exalted above all else in worship, preaching, and teaching?
- Observe: Do sermons align with Scripture, or are they based on opinions and culture?
- Test: Does this church lead people into a deeper relationship with Christ?

2. Accountable Leadership

A church should reflect Jesus, not a pastor-centered culture. If a church revolves around one leader's charisma rather than Christ's authority, that's a red flag. A healthy church has leaders who serve with humility, transparency, and accountability. They do not abuse their authority but lead with integrity, following Christ's example.

Hebrews 13:17 *"Have confidence in your leaders and submit to their authority, because they keep watch over you as those who must give an account."*

- Observe how leadership interacts with the congregation. Do they serve humbly, or do they demand blind loyalty?
- Ask if leadership is held accountable. Is there a board or elder team providing oversight?
- Look for financial transparency. Are financial decisions openly communicated?
- Test their humility. Do they accept correction, or do they reject accountability.

3. Grace-Filled Environment

A healthy church does not operate in shame or fear but in grace. The focus should be on redemption, not condemnation. Jesus modeled grace and truth **(John 1:14)**. A church that is legalistic, fear-based, or quick to judge is not reflecting the heart of Christ.

Romans 8:1 *"There is now no condemnation for those who are in Christ Jesus."*

- Observe how the church responds to those who struggle. Are people met with love, encouragement, and restoration?
- Ask yourself: Do you feel free to be honest about your struggles, or do you feel the need to pretend?
- Pay attention to how mistakes are handled. Are members shamed publicly, or are they guided toward healing?

4. Encouragement to Grow

A church should not control your spiritual journey—it should equip and encourage you to grow in Christ. Jesus invited people to grow in their faith—He never forced them into blind obedience. A healthy church nurtures growth without fear or control.

2 Peter 3:18 *"Grow in the grace and knowledge of our Lord and Savior Jesus Christ."*

- Look for a church that teaches biblical truth without manipulation. Do they encourage personal study, or do they discourage questioning?
- Engage in discipleship opportunities. Does the church offer Bible studies, mentorship, and ways to grow deeper in faith?
- Ask if it is safe to ask questions. Are people encouraged to explore their faith, or are they expected to follow without thinking?

5. Genuine Relationships

A Spirit-filled church should feel like family—united in Christ, walking together in love, and committed to supporting one another. Church is not just about services and sermons—it is about real, Spirit-filled relationships.

John 13:35 *"By this everyone will know that you are my disciples, if you love one another."*

- Engage in conversation. Are people welcoming and genuinely interested in connecting with you?
- Observe church culture. Do people build each other up in love, or is there gossip and division?
- Ask yourself: Can I see myself forming real, God-honoring friendships here?

Why Church still Matters

Walking in faith was never meant to be a lonely journey. The enemy would love for you to believe you're better off alone, but God designed us for community. A healthy, Christ-centered church should be a place of growth, healing, and encouragement—where believers uplift one another and draw closer to Him together.

God will lead you to the right community in His time. Trust Him.

Trying a church again may not happen instantly, and that's okay. You don't have to rush. Healing takes time, and finding a church home where you feel safe, seen, and spiritually fed is a process. You may visit several places before you sense God's peace confirming, *"This is it."* Don't be discouraged if it takes a few tries—each step is part of your journey, and none of it is wasted.

Give yourself permission to explore with open hands and an open heart. Take note of how you feel when you're there—do you sense the Holy Spirit's presence? Is there peace? Are people welcoming, authentic, and humble? Does the leadership operate with transparency and grace? These are good signs of a healthy, Christ-centered community.

And if you don't find that right away, don't lose hope. You're not being picky—you're being discerning. The church, when it reflects the heart of Jesus, is a beautiful, powerful thing. God desires that you be planted in a place where your soul can thrive. He will lead you there in His perfect time.

You don't have to go back to what hurt you. You're moving toward something better. Trust that God is preparing the right people, the right place, and the right moment to restore what was broken—with even greater joy and deeper faith than before.

Freedom is Ahead!

Your pain is not the end of your story—God is still writing it. There is a church family waiting for you, a place where you will experience healing, freedom, and growth in Christ.

A Christ-centered church isn't just a building or a routine—it's a place of transformation, a community where you can step into the fullness of God's love and purpose for your life.

"Commit your way to the Lord; trust in Him, and He will do this." **Psalm 37:5**

Hold on to hope. Freedom, healing, and renewal are ahead!

Trusting God in the Process

Finding the right church takes time, and the journey may feel uncertain—but God is faithful. He knows your needs, your wounds, and your desire to find a community rooted in His truth and grace. You don't have to figure it all out at once.

Isaiah 26:3-4 reminds us: *"You will keep in perfect peace those whose minds are steadfast, because they trust in you. Trust in the Lord forever, for the Lord, the Lord himself, is the Rock eternal."*

Finding the right church takes time, and it's okay if you don't have all the answers yet. What matters is that you're taking the first step. Ask God for wisdom, do your research, visit with discernment, and trust that He will guide you to a community that reflects His love, truth, and grace. You don't have to rush or settle. The same God who has walked with you through healing will also lead you into restoration. Let this next step be taken in peace—not pressure—and with full confidence that God is preparing a place for you to grow, belong, and thrive.

Prayer Space

Take a moment to write a prayer below. Ask God for wisdom, peace, and confidence in this next season of finding a healthy, Christ-centered community.

Lord, I invite *You* into this process…

_____

_____

_____

_____

_____

_____

_____

_____

_____

Reflection Questions:

1. What qualities are most important to you in a new faith community?

Answer: _____

_____

_____

_____

2. How can you actively engage in building healthier relationships within your new community?

Answer: _____

_____

_____

_____

3. What fears or reservations do you have about rejoining a church, and how can you address them?

Answer: _____

_____

_____

_____

Biblical Encouragement:

Proverbs 27:17 "As iron sharpens iron, so one person sharpens another."

Galatians 6:2 "Carry each other's burdens, and in this way, you will fulfill the law of Christ."

John 13:34-35 "Love one another. As I have loved you, so you must love one another."

Journaling Exercise: Defining a Healthy Faith Community

1. What are the key qualities you want in a new church or faith community?

Answer: _____

_____

_____

_____

2. What are red flags you will look out for in a new spiritual environment?

Answer: _____

_____

_____

_____

3. How can you remain open to finding genuine fellowship while protecting yourself from past patterns?

Answer: _____

_____

_____

_____

Prayer for Guidance in Finding Community

Father, I surrender my wounds to You. Heal my heart and restore my faith. Lead me into a church community that reflects Your love, truth, and grace. Amen.

Practical Checklists for Key Steps

These checklists are designed to help you take practical steps toward healing and growth. Use them as a guide to track your progress and stay intentional about your journey.

Checklist: Evaluating a Healthy Church Community

✔ Does the leadership demonstrate accountability and humility? ☐

✔ Is there a culture of grace rather than fear-based control? ☐

✔ Are questions welcomed, or is blind loyalty expected? ☐

✔ Does the church encourage personal growth in faith? ☐

✔ Is there transparency in financial and operational matters? ☐

✔ Do relationships feel genuine and Christ-centered? ☐

Journaling & Prayer Reflection

At the end of each chapter, take a moment to pause and reflect. Use this space to write down what stood out to you, what emotions you experienced, and any insights God has revealed to you. Feel free to write a personal prayer, expressing your thoughts, gratitude, or requests for healing.

Reflection & Journaling

Journaling Prompt:

What step from the checklist do you have the most trouble discerning?

_____

_____

_____

_____

_____

Who could help you with this at a new church?

_____

_____

_____

_____

_____

Notes & Reflections:

(Use this space to write thoughts, prayers, or anything on your heart.)

_____

_____

_____

_____

_____

_____

_____

_____

_____

_____

_____

_____

_____

_____

_____

_____

_____

_____

Prayer Space

Write a personal prayer for this season of your life. Ask God for wisdom, healing, or strength to continue your journey.

_____

_____

_____

_____

_____

_____

_____

_____

_____

Spiritual Reset: God Provides Community

Take a moment to pause and recenter. Let this Scripture speak truth and peace over your heart before moving forward.

*Scripture: **Hebrews 10:24-25** "Let us consider how we may spur one another on toward love and good deeds, not giving up meeting together."*

Chapter 5 Scripture Summary

Acts 2:42: "*They devoted themselves to the apostles' teaching and to fellowship, to the breaking of bread and to prayer.*"

Ecclesiastes 4:9-10: "*Two are better than one, because they have a good return for their labor: If either of them falls down, one can help the other up. But pity anyone who falls and has no one to help them up.*"

Colossians 1:18: "*And he is the head of the body, the church; he is the beginning and the firstborn from among the dead, so that in everything he might have the supremacy.*"

Hebrews 13:17: "*Have confidence in your leaders and submit to their authority, because they keep watch over you as those who must give an account. Do this so that their work will be a joy, not a burden, for that would be of no benefit to you.*"

John 1:14: "*The Word became flesh and made his dwelling among us. We have seen his glory, the glory of the one and only Son, who came from the Father, full of grace and truth.*"

Romans 8:1: "*Therefore, there is now no condemnation for those who are in Christ Jesus.*"

2 Peter 3:18: "*But grow in the grace and knowledge of our Lord and Savior Jesus Christ. To him be glory both now and forever! Amen.*"

John 13:35: "*By this everyone will know that you are my disciples, if you love one another.*"

Psalm 37:5: "*Commit your way to the Lord; trust in him and he will do this.*"

Isaiah 26:3-4: "*You will keep in perfect peace those whose minds are steadfast, because they trust in you. Trust in the Lord forever, for the Lord, the Lord himself, is the Rock eternal.*"

Hebrews 10:24-25: "*And let us consider how we may spur one another on toward love and good deeds, not giving up meeting together, as some are in the habit of doing, but encouraging one another—and all the more as you see the Day approaching.*"

Proverbs 27:17: "*As iron sharpens iron, so a friend sharpens a friend.*"

Galatians 6:2: "*Share each other's burdens, and in this way obey the law of Christ.*"

John 13:34–35: "*So now I am giving you a new commandment: Love each other. Just as I have loved you, you should love each other. Your love for one another will prove to the world that you are my disciples.*"

Philippians 1:6: "*And I am certain that God, who began the good work within you, will continue his work until it is finally finished on the day when Christ Jesus returns.*"

Romans 12:10: "*Love each other with genuine affection, and take delight in honoring each other.*"

The Healing Journey: A Path to Freedom in Christ

This journey doesn't happen all at once—and it rarely follows a straight line. But every step you've taken matters. Whether you're just beginning to ask questions or stepping into a renewed church community, let this visual be a reminder that healing, rebuilding, and rediscovering your faith after spiritual pain is a sacred and grace-filled process.

Your Healing Journey

A visual path to restoration in Christ

Healing is seldom a straightforward journey. Some days may feel like significant progress, while others might seem stagnant. And that's perfectly fine. This is not a checklist—it's a gentle reminder that healing is a sacred experience. No matter your stage—whether you're just starting, processing emotions, or rebuilding—God is by your side. Let this journey map inspire you to contemplate your past, recognize your present, and envision where He is guiding you next.

Heal, Rebuild Your Faith, and Rediscover Christ-Centered Community

Step one Recognizing	Step two Leaving	Step three Healing	Step four Rebuilding	Final Step Community

Step 1: Recognizing the Red Flags

- You begin to notice what doesn't reflect the heart of Jesus

Step 2: Leaving with Peace

- You take a courageous step to walk away seeking God's truth and freedom.

Step 3: Healing the Wounds

- You grieve, reflect, and process with God.

Step 4: Rebuilding Your Faith

- Your faith is no longer tied to a building or a leader—it's rooted in Christ alone.

Step 5: Rediscovering Community

- You find safe spaces to grow again—places marked by truth and spiritual health.

Final Thoughts: Faith Beyond Toxicity

Leaving a toxic church is not the end of your faith—it can be the beginning of a deeper, healthier relationship with Jesus.

If you've been hurt by the church, know this: God's love is not defined by human failures. As you take steps forward, trust that He is leading you toward a faith that is authentic, life-giving, and unshaken.

You are stepping into a season of renewal. The past does not define you—God does. Keep moving forward. He has something greater ahead.

Biblical Encouragement:

Isaiah 43:19 "See, I am doing a new thing! Now it springs up; do you not perceive it? I am making a way in the wilderness and streams in the wasteland."

Philippians 1:6 "Being confident of this, that he who began a good work in you will carry it on to completion until the day of Christ Jesus."

Romans 12:10 "Be devoted to one another in love. Honor one another above yourselves."

Prayer for Peace, Guidance and Godly Community

Father, I come before You with a heart in need of healing. I lay down the pain, confusion, and fear I've carried, and I ask for Your peace to calm my spirit. Fill the places that feel broken with Your presence. Lead me with Your wisdom, and help me to walk in confidence, knowing You are guiding every step I take.

Lord, I surrender the wounds I've experienced in the church—both seen and unseen. I ask that You soften my heart and help me release bitterness and mistrust. Teach me to forgive without returning to what hurt me. Restore my hope in what community can be when You are truly at the center.

Lead me to a body of believers who reflect Your love—those willing to walk with me in truth, grace, and encouragement.—people who will walk with me in truth, grace, and encouragement. Place me in a church family that carries one another's burdens, sharpens one another in faith, and seeks Your face above all else. Heal what's been broken, restore what's been lost, and use my life as a vessel for Your love and healing in return.

In Jesus' name, Amen

Notes & Reflections:

(Use this space to write thoughts or anything on your heart.)

_____

_____

_____

_____

_____

_____

_____

_____

_____

_____

_____

_____

_____

_____

_____

_____

_____

_____

Frequently Asked Questions

How do I explain my decision to leave to friends and family?

Be honest but firm. You don't have to defend your decision, but you can share how it aligns with your spiritual well-being.

One example could be:

"This church no longer supports my spiritual well-being so I have decided to go somewhere else that does."

Some people won't understand, and that's okay. Prioritize your healing over pleasing others.

What if I feel guilty for leaving?

Recognize that guilt is often a result of manipulation. Leaving a toxic church is not leaving God.

God desires freedom, truth, and love—not coercion or fear-based obedience.

How do I handle Church members who try to convince me to stay?

Set clear boundaries. A simple "I appreciate your concern, but I've already made up my mind."

Avoid engaging in arguments. You don't need to justify your choice.

How Do I Know If a New Church Is Healthy?

A healthy church is rooted in **truth, love, and spiritual maturity**. It won't be perfect—but it will reflect the character of Christ in its culture, leadership, and relationships.

Transparency

Transparency means the church leadership is open and honest about how things are run. This includes:

- Clearly communicated **financial practices** (budget, giving, stewardship)

- **Decision-making processes** that include accountability, not secrecy

- Open conversations about doctrine, mission, and vision

- Willingness to address hard topics like leadership failures, reconciliation, or sin—without covering them up

Transparency builds trust. In a healthy church, **nothing important is hidden** from the people who are part of the community.

Accountability

Accountability means that **no one is above correction or counsel**—even pastors and leaders. In a healthy church:

- Leaders are **submitted to elders, boards, or outside counsel**

- Pastors don't operate in isolation—they're surrounded by spiritual oversight

- Members are encouraged to **grow in character and truth**, not out of fear, but out of love and spiritual responsibility

- Conflicts or concerns are handled biblically, not defensively or with retaliation

Accountability **protects both the leaders and the congregation** from abuse, pride, and manipulation.

A Culture of Grace vs. a Culture of Control

A healthy church creates an atmosphere where **grace leads**—not fear.

A **grace-filled Church**:

- Welcomes your questions and doesn't shame you for asking them

- Encourages spiritual growth at **your pace**, not under pressure

- Responds to failure with **restoration**, not humiliation

- Reminds you of your **identity in Christ**, not your performance

A **controlling Church**:

- Uses fear, guilt, or shame to keep people in line

- Makes loyalty to leadership more important than obedience to God

- Discourages independent thought or personal discernment

- Threatens consequences for "disobedience" rather than pointing to freedom in Christ

Jesus came to set you free—not to place you under spiritual bondage. A healthy church will reflect His heart.

Self-Assessment Quiz: Where Am I in My Healing Journey?

Take a moment to reflect on your healing process by answering the questions below. Choose the response that best describes how you currently feel.

1. Do I still feel guilty for leaving my old church?
A. No, I feel like there is a clean break from my past church.
B. Yes, but I recognize it's false guilt and I'm working through it.
C. Yes, because I left others behind.
D. Yes, I can't stop thinking about it and it weighs on me often.

2. Am I struggling to trust another church community?
A. No, I feel open to trusting again when the time is right.
B. I have some hesitation, but I know not all churches are the same.
C. I want to trust again but feel unsure and guarded.
D. Yes, I don't believe I'll ever trust a church again.

3. Have I been able to separate God from my church experience?
A. Yes, I know God is not the same as what I experienced.
B. I'm learning to see God more clearly apart from the church.
C. Sometimes—I still associate God with the pain.
D. Not really—I feel distant from God because of the hurt I experienced from church.

4. Do I feel closer to healing, or do I feel stuck?
A. I feel freer and more at peace with each step forward.
B. I've made progress, but I still have difficult moments.
C. I feel stuck and unsure of how to move forward.
D. I feel like I haven't started healing at all.

5. Have I forgiven those who hurt me, or am I holding onto bitterness?
A. I've forgiven them and feel released from the burden.
B. I'm working on forgiveness and feel it happening gradually.
C. I still feel resentment, but I want to let it go.
D. I don't think I can forgive them yet.

6. What steps have I taken toward finding a new faith community?
A. I've visited or found a new community where I feel safe.
B. I'm exploring slowly and trying to stay open.
C. I haven't taken steps yet, but I want to.
D. I avoid churches and have no plans to return.

Interpreting Your Responses

- **Mostly A's** – You're walking in **a healthy direction**. You've processed much of your past, and you're positioned for continued healing and growth.

- **Mostly B's** – You're **headed in the right direction**, but still need encouragement and time. Be gentle with yourself—progress is still progress.

- **Mostly C's** – You're **aware of your pain**, but healing may still feel out of reach. Keep leaning into God's love and consider opening up to trusted support.

- **Mostly D's** – You may feel **deeply wounded or stuck**, and that's okay. This might be a good time to seek out a **Christian counselor, support group, or trusted mentor** to walk with you.

Reflection Space:

What did this quiz reveal about your heart?

_____

_____

_____

_____

_____

_____

_____

_____

_____

_____

_____

_____

_____

Remember: God is not rushing your healing. He meets you exactly where you are—with compassion, not pressure. Whatever stage you're in, **He's walking with you, guiding you one step at a time.**

Emergency Scriptures for Strength and Comfort

Peace in Anxiety

Philippians 4:6-7: "Do not be anxious about anything, but in every situation, by prayer and petition, with thanksgiving, present your requests to God. And the peace of God, which transcends all understanding, will guard your hearts and your minds in Christ Jesus."

Strength in Weakness

Isaiah 40:31: "But those who hope in the Lord will renew their strength. They will soar on wings like eagles; they will run and not grow weary, they will walk and not be faint."

Encouragement When Feeling Alone

Deuteronomy 31:8: "The Lord himself goes before you and will be with you; he will never leave you nor forsake you. Do not be afraid; do not be discouraged."

Healing from Heartbreak

Matthew 5:4: "Blessed are those who mourn, for they will be comforted."

Trusting God's Plan

Romans 15:13: "May the God of hope fill you with all joy and peace as you trust in Him, so that you may overflow with hope by the power of the Holy Spirit."

Finding Rest in God

Psalm 55:22: "Cast your cares on the Lord and he will sustain you; he will never let the righteous be shaken."

Overcoming Fear

Joshua 1:9: "Have I not commanded you? Be strong and courageous. Do not be afraid; do not be discouraged, for the Lord your God will be with you wherever you go."

Hope in Trials

Romans 8:28: "And we know that in all things God works for the good of those who love Him, who have been called according to His purpose."

Study Group Guide

This book can be used individually or in a study group setting. Healing from church wounds are often best processed with the support of trusted friends, mentors, or a small group. This guide provides a structured approach for group discussions and encourages open, prayerful conversations as you walk through the journey of healing together.

How to Use This Study Group Guide

1. Meet Weekly

Set aside time each week to go through a chapter together. Creating consistency allows for deeper reflection, accountability, and encouragement. Whether meeting in person, through a video call, or in a group chat, regular meetings will help foster connection and growth.

2. Open in Prayer

Begin each session with prayer, inviting the Holy Spirit to guide your discussion. Ask for wisdom, clarity, and healing for everyone in the group. If anyone has specific prayer requests related to their journey, this is a great time to lift those up.

3. Read the Chapter Summary

Each week, have one person give a brief summary of the assigned chapter. This helps reinforce key themes and ensures that everyone is on the same page. If someone missed a reading, this also provides an opportunity for them to catch up.

4. Discuss Reflection Questions

The provided discussion questions will help guide your conversation. Encourage open and honest sharing, but also respect each person's comfort level. If certain topics feel too personal, it's okay to reflect internally. The goal is to create a space where healing and growth can happen.

5. Journaling & Sharing (Optional)

Each chapter includes prompts for personal reflection. If participants feel comfortable, they can share insights from their journaling time. This practice can deepen conversations and help others relate to different experiences. However, journaling is personal, and sharing should always be optional.

6. Apply What You've Learned

End each session by discussing how to apply what you've learned in daily life. What action steps can you take this week? How can you walk in healing, set boundaries, or grow closer to God? Close the meeting with prayer, asking for strength and wisdom to continue the journey.

Study Group Enhancements

For those using this book in a group setting, here are additional tools.

Icebreaker Questions

What led you to read this book?

What is one thing you hope to gain from this study?

What flag led you to question or leave your church?

Weekly Challenges for Study Groups

These weekly challenges provide **practical steps** for reflection, healing, and growth.

Week 1 (Chapter 1: Recognizing a Toxic Church Culture)

Challenge: Write down three specific moments when you felt uneasy in a church setting. Reflect on how those experiences shaped your faith and discuss with the group how to recognize red flags.

Week 2 (Chapter 2: The Emotional & Spiritual Impact of Leaving)

Challenge: Consider the emotions you've experienced since leaving your church. Choose one emotion (grief, guilt, relief, anger, etc.) and bring it before God in prayer, asking for clarity and healing.

Week 3 (Chapter 3: Steps to Leaving an Unhealthy Church)

Challenge: Create a "boundary statement." Write out a short paragraph about what you will and will not allow in future church environments. Share it with a trusted friend or group member for encouragement.

Week 4 (Chapter 4: Time to Heal)

Challenge: Pray for someone who hurt you in a church setting. You don't have to reach out to them, but spend time asking God to help you release any bitterness and move forward in healing.

Week 5 (Chapter 5: Finding a Healthy Church Community)

Challenge: Research and visit a new church (in-person or online). Observe how it makes you feel—does it reflect the values discussed in this book? If you're not ready to visit, spend time praying for God to guide you toward the right community.

Chapter-by-Chapter Discussion Questions

Chapter 1: When Church Culture Becomes Harmful

✔ What are some red flags you've noticed in church leadership?

✔ How can we encourage spiritual accountability in churches today?

✔ What did this chapter reveal to you about your own faith journey?

Chapter 2: The Emotional & Spiritual Impact of Leaving

✔ What emotions have you struggled with after leaving a toxic church?

✔ How has leaving impacted your relationship with God?

✔ What steps have helped (or could help) you heal spiritually and emotionally?

Chapter 3: Steps to Leaving an unhealthy Church

✔ What was the most challenging part of deciding to leave?

✔ What practical steps can someone take to leave well?

✔ How can we support someone who is struggling with this decision?

Chapter 4: Healing Church Wounds

✔ What role does forgiveness play in healing from spiritual abuse?

✔ Who is God calling you to forgive and why?

✔ What have you found most helpful in your healing process?

Chapter 5: Finding a Healthy Church Community

✔ What are key characteristics of a healthy church?

✔ What steps can you take to find a faith community that aligns with biblical principles?

✔ How can we rebuild trust in church leadership after experiencing church hurt?

Final Encouragement for Study Groups

This journey is not just about healing—it's about rediscovering the true love and gentleness of Christ, often hidden beneath the wounds of spiritual hurt. Whether your group has laughed, cried, wrestled with hard truths, or sat in silent reflection, know that your presence here matters. Every page you've worked through and every conversation you've shared is a step toward healing, wholeness, and deeper intimacy with God.

Take your time. Be patient with the process—and with each other. Some may still be in the thick of grief, while others are beginning to feel the first signs of peace and renewal. That's okay. God works in all of us at different rhythms, and He is faithful to complete what He started in each heart **(Philippians 1:6).**

Let this study continue to be a safe place:
 A place where honesty is welcomed, not judged.
 A place where grace is given freely.
 A place where truth is spoken in love and received with humility.
 A place where healing is possible, even in the presence of pain. The church is not perfect—but Christ is. And He is calling each of you into something deeper, something freer, and something more beautiful than what you've left behind. As a group, may you grow together in wisdom, discernment, and bold compassion—not just for yourselves, but for the Body of Christ as a whole.

Keep showing up. Keep seeking Jesus. Keep holding space for one another. You are not walking this road alone—and the healing He has for you will overflow into the lives of others.

You're part of a greater restoration story. Let it unfold—together.

Where to Go from Here

Healing is an ongoing journey, and finding the right support is essential. Below are some general resources to guide you:

Christian Counseling & Support

Seeking professional counseling from a faith-based perspective can be helpful. Consider looking for:

- Licensed Christian counselors who align with your values.
- Biblical counseling services that offer emotional and spiritual guidance.
- Support groups or online communities focused on healing from difficult church experiences.

Books on Healing & Spiritual Growth

Reading about others' experiences and insights can provide wisdom and encouragement. Consider books on:

- Recognizing and recovering from unhealthy church dynamics.
- Building and fostering spiritually healthy communities.
- Understanding biblical leadership, accountability, and healing.

Finding a Healthy Church Community

If you're searching for a new place to grow spiritually, these steps may help:

- Look for church communities that prioritize biblical teaching, transparency, and accountability.
- Explore church directories or visit local congregations to find a supportive and healthy environment.
- Seek recommendations from trusted friends or mentors.

About the Author

Victoria Russo is a certified biblical counselor and ministry leader with a passion for helping the spiritually wounded find healing, clarity, and restoration through the truth of God's Word.

With years of experience mentoring women, leading Bible studies, and walking alongside others through faith-related challenges, Victoria creates resources that blend biblical truth with compassionate guidance. She wrote *Leaving Well, Healing Deep* to help those navigating church hurt, spiritual confusion, or unhealthy church environments find hope and renewed trust in Christ.

Her *Faith After Church Hurt* series also includes a **21-day healing devotional** and a **21-day companion journal**—designed to support others in their healing journey one step at a time.

Today, she continues to serve through *Truthwoven Ministries*, offering devotionals, Bible studies, and Christ-centered tools that equip believers for lasting healing and spiritual growth.

Discover more at: www.truthwovenministries.org

Complete Scripture Index